The Warrior Mom's Guide to Single Motherhood by Choice

Reclaiming Peace, Health, and Wholeness After Carrying It All

Author Shaundra M. G. Harris

The Warrior Mom's Guide to Single Motherhood by Choice

Reclaiming Peace, Health, and Wholeness After Carrying It All

Author Shaundra M. G. Harris

Shaun The Mom Publishing

© 2025 Shaundra M. G. Harris

All rights reserved.

Paperback ISBN: 978-1-969446-04-7
Hardback ISBN: 978-1-969446-14-6

First Edition

No part of this publication may be reproduced, stored in a retrieval system, or transmitted in any form without written permission from the author, except by reviewers or educators using brief quotations with proper citation.

Shaun The Mom Publishing

Printed in the United States.

www.warriormomacademy.com

Disclaimer

This book is intended for informational and inspirational purposes only. The content reflects the personal experiences, opinions, and insights of the author and should not be considered a substitute for professional medical, legal, financial, educational, therapeutic, or spiritual advice.

While the author shares tools, tips, and resources that have been personally helpful, every situation is unique. Readers are encouraged to consult with qualified professionals before making decisions regarding health, finances, homeschooling, parenting, estate planning, or other matters discussed in this book.

Some links or references provided may be affiliate links. This means the author may receive a small commission at no extra cost to you if you choose to purchase through those links. These recommendations are made in good faith and only include resources the author personally uses or believes may be helpful.

Any printable templates, checklists, or workbook materials included are for personal use only and may not be distributed, sold, or used commercially without written permission from the author.

The author and publisher expressly disclaim any liability arising directly or indirectly from the use or misuse of any information, tools, or resources included in this book.

To my babies. Aoki, Layla, Jayden and Nia. Let's live our best lives.

And I'm sorry it took me so long.

Welcome

There comes a moment in every warrior woman's life when she's faced with a choice: Should I stay, or should I go?

That question wears many faces—marriage, partnership, motherhood, friendships, even family—and each version comes with very real consequences.

If I stay...

- I may continue to suffer.
- I may remain stuck in cycles of pain, disappointment, and survival.
- I'll likely still feel unseen, unheard, unsupported, and unappreciated.

If I go...

- I'll have to do life alone—raise the kids, pay the bills, face the loneliness.
- I'll have no help during sickness or setbacks.
- I'll have to walk through healing without a partner beside me.

But here's what I discovered: Whatever brought you to the question doesn't matter as much as the realization that follows: "I can't keep living like this."

That's when the choice becomes clear. That's when change begins.

Table of Contents

Introduction *2*
    Why I Wrote This Book 2
    My Choice to Be Single 3
    From Survival to Self-Love 10
    Choosing Self-Love and Single Motherhood .. 17

Part I: Naming the Truth *20*
    Chapter 1: When You're Already the One Doing Everything 21
    Chapter 2: The Myth of Help 25
    Chapter 3: Chronic Illness as a Catalyst 30
    Chapter 4: The Moment You Decide: No More Pretending 35

Part II: Reclaiming Your Life *40*
    Chapter 5: Housing as Freedom 41
    Chapter 6: Financial Foundations 46
    Chapter 7: Legal and Practical Protections ... 52

Part III: Healing from the Past *57*
    Chapter 8: Grieving What You Thought You Had 58
    Chapter 9: Releasing Guilt and Shame 62
    Chapter 10: Rebuilding Your Identity 67
    Chapter 11: Reconnecting with God and Your Spirit 72

Part IV: Thriving as a Single Mother by Choice *77*

Chapter 12: Redefining Success on Your Terms 78

Chapter 13: Building a Home That Heals 83

Chapter 14: Raising Whole, Resilient Children 88

Chapter 15: Moms Raising Daughters........... 92

Chapter 16: Moms Raising Sons 97

Chapter 17: Cultivating Joy and Purpose 102

Part V: Staying the Course...................... 107

Chapter 18: Navigating Setbacks Without Losing Ground 108

Chapter 19: Protecting Your Peace and Setting Boundaries 113

Chapter 20: Cultivating a Support Village ... 117

Part VI: Growing Into Your New Self...... 123

Chapter 21: Growing Into Your New Self 124

Chapter 22: Embracing the Future with Intention..129

Chapter 23: Setting Goals That Matter to You 133

Chapter 24: Teaching Your Children Resilience and Love 137

Chapter 25: Leaving a Legacy of Strength and Faith 142

Chapter 26: This Is Just the Beginning 146

Closing Thoughts 150

Scriptures for Strength & Provision..........152

About the Author *153*

The Warrior Mom's Guide™ Book Series 154

Acknowledgments *157*

Resource List *158*

Reflection Journals & Worksheets *159*

Introduction

Why I Wrote This Book

This book is for the woman at her breaking point.

The one caught in the middle of staying and going.

The one who's scared, sick, and tired—literally and figuratively.

I wrote this for the warrior mama who knows there's more but isn't sure if she can make it alone.

Let me be living proof:

You can.

With God, guidance, and grit—you absolutely can.

Jesus is the way out, and the way through.

You're not just single by circumstance—you can be Single By Choice.

And when you choose yourself, you're not choosing loneliness—you're choosing life.

Let's walk this out together.

My Choice to Be Single

My decision to become single didn't come from strength—it came from survival.

Honestly, I probably just needed a hug. And I got one—a big, overwhelming bear hug from God.

But it wasn't soft or sweet at first. It was tight. So tight it left me breathless, cracked a few ribs (figuratively), and made me pass out emotionally and spiritually more than once. Yet when I finally came to, I exhaled for the first time in years. I let go of the trauma, the stress, and the survival mode I had called "life."

For over twenty years, I was in two back-to-back relationships. The first lasted seven years. The second, nearly thirteen. Because there was less then a month in between relationships, and they nearly overlapped, there were rumors—but they were unrelated.

Even so, in both relationships, I had one foot out the door long before I left. And still, I stayed. Hoping to make things work. But nope.

I tolerated too much. I sacrificed too much. But here's the truth: people only do what you allow.

I allowed it. Whether out of fear, survival, safety, provision, or just not wanting to start over—I stayed.

I shared my life, my love, my body, and my vision. I tried to build families, but it cost me everything, including my health. What looked like partnership on the outside felt like imprisonment on the inside.

The Breaking Point

With my second relationship, I didn't arrive at my break-up decision easily, it was more of an emergency landing.

To avoid a complete wreck.

After quite a few turbulent years and multiple infidelities, a series of lies and abandonment, I eventually came face to face with that lovely question. The one that changed my life forever:

Should I stay, or should I go?

If I stay...

- I will continue to be sick.
- I'll continue to struggle financially and emotionally.
- I'll remain invisible and voiceless.
- I'll carry everything on my back while being lied to, cheated on, and disrespected.
- He will not change.
- He doesn't even like me.

- And I'm already doing everything alone.

If I go (or make him go)...

- I'll still have to raise the kids alone.
- Pay the bills alone.
- Go to the doctor alone.
- Pick myself up when I fall—alone.
- Homeschool, handle appointments, and life—alone.

But guess what? I was already doing it all alone. Whether he was on the road for work or home but still unavailable. I was doing it all. The only thing he added to my life was stress, heartbreak, and medical crises.

When Stress Makes You Sick

Living with sickle cell disease, I can't afford emotional chaos.

My health is directly tied to my mental and emotional well-being. Stress, negativity, and toxicity can literally send me into a painful, dangerous crisis.

I realized I wasn't just heartbroken—I was physically allergic to the environment I was in.

I was choosing sickness by choosing him.

So I chose me.

The Decision That Saved My Life

After nearly a month-long hospital stay—alone, weak, and uncertain—I made a decision:

"If I have to be alone in the darkest valley of my life, I'd rather also be alone at the mountaintop."

That relationship didn't end immediately.

There was back-and-forth, lies and tries, false starts and tears. But eventually, God gave me the strength to break free.

Now, after over four years of being single, I can honestly say:

it was the best decision I ever made.

The Gift of Singleness

Every area of my life has changed for the better.

I'm not saying all this to paint him as the worst man I've ever known—but if I'm being honest, he and that other one are definitely in the top two.

I say this because I was just fifteen and a half when I got into my first relationship. By sixteen, I had moved in with a grown man and dropped out of school. I went through every kind of abuse with him—physical, emotional, and financial. It took courage and a bit of cleverness to get out of that situation, only to find myself in another kind of prison not long after.

The truth is, I've never had time to just be me—for me. To love myself for the sake of growing into a woman.

I've always had a toxic or negative home life, both as a child and as an adult. So living on my own, making all the decisions, taking full responsibility, and doing so without interference, ego, or battles—that was a first.

This time of singleness has given me the space to get to know God and to build an empire—a legacy—for my children. (And that only took a year!)

I've had space to heal, time to grow, and peace to breathe. I've drawn closer to God and to my children. I've lost nearly 100 pounds, and my finances are improving.

The silence—without a negative voice in your ear—is a rare and beautiful kind of sanity. My life has improved in every way, and I believe what's coming next will only get better.

🦋 Reflection | Affirmation | Prayer | Action

My Choice to Be Single

Reflection Questions

1. Have you ever stayed in a relationship because it felt safer than being alone?
2. What was the moment you knew, deep down, that things would never change?
3. What would freedom look like for you right now—if you were brave enough to choose it?

Affirmation

"I choose peace over chaos. I choose health over heartbreak. I choose me."

Prayer

Lord, help me to see myself the way You see me—worthy, loved, and whole.

Give me the courage to release what harms me and the faith to believe You have more for me. Amen.

Action Step

Take a few minutes to write down why you are reading this book.

- What are you hoping to find here?
- What are you ready to release?
- What are you ready to build?

Keep this page somewhere safe. Let it serve as your first commitment—to yourself.

From Survival to Self-Love

I never set out to become a single mother by choice.

Not in the way most people think of it—using a donor, planning solo parenthood from the start.

My choice came from a deeper place. A place of exhaustion. Of finally acknowledging that, even when I was in relationships, I was alone.

Two long partnerships—seven years and nearly thirteen years—left me doing all the work.

The labor of building a home, caring for children, and holding everything together while receiving none of the safety or partnership I deserved.

Living with chronic illness, sickle cell anemia, shaped my journey in ways many people will never understand. Fatigue, pain, and the constant fear of my body giving out made stability feel like a distant dream.

But in the midst of that struggle, I learned something that changed my life:

If I was going to carry everything alone anyway, I might as well do it on my own terms.

The First Relationship: Losing Myself Young

I met my first "not-husband" when I was fifteen, almost sixteen.

I was just a teenager at the mall with my cousin when this older guy approached me. He told me he had just turned eighteen, worked at a bank, and had his own apartment. He seemed like he had it all together—more than any boy I knew at school.

But he wasn't eighteen. He was twenty-two. I didn't know that until I had already committed to him, until after I lost my virginity under the promise that we'd be married when I turned eighteen.

By the time I learned the truth, I was too deep in it—living in his apartment, cut off from my family, too embarrassed and ashamed to leave.

He made me drop out of high school, convinced me my family wouldn't take me back, and kept me dependent on him.

For years, I was an unpaid maid, a cook, and a prisoner to his insecurities. He took most of my paychecks. He tracked who I talked to. He used my youth and my lack of experience to control me.

When all his manipulations stopped working—when I finally stopped caring—he turned violent.

That was the final line he crossed.

He put his hands around my throat, trying to break what was left of my spirit.

But even in that darkness, something in me refused to die. I fought back with everything I had (and a cast iron skillet).

That moment landed me in jail, broke what little was left of our relationship, and marked the beginning of my first plan to get away and save myself.

The Second Relationship: Trading One Cage for Another

I thought the second relationship would be different.

I was older, working, finding my independence again. But I still hadn't learned how to spot the same cycle in a different body.

He started with love bombing—promises of marriage, family, security. I was tired, vulnerable, and raising my first child. Everyone around me told me to "give him a chance," so I did.

Years went by in that second "not marriage." More financial abuse. More infidelity. More excuses.

He moved out of his apartment and into my townhouse, so we could live together and stack money. It never sat right with me not being married and then he proposed. So we set a date to marry at the courthouse. After spending the day getting ready and arriving at the courthouse, he backed out right in front of the courthouse.

But we lied to everyone—said we were married—because the shame of failure was too heavy to face. He didn't know it, but he lost me on so many levels that day.

After challenges between my work life and family life, I could no longer work. I became a stay-at-home mom by default, homeschooling, budgeting, and carrying the load for everyone. I planned and managed all our lives, our bills, while he squandered money and time.

When he got a better job, he basically told me my contributions didn't matter. After budgeting and planning I managed to save our household over $1,000, when I started suggesting all the things we could do with the money like start a savings since we were paycheck to paycheck, he remarked:

> "How are you going to sit here and spend my money?"
> He bought speakers.

That was the moment I knew—if I didn't make a plan for my life, nothing would ever change. I later got a job working the night shift at a hospital's coffee shop. Something was better than nothing.

The Final Awakening

The final push came when my health broke down again. A family vacation turned into a medical crisis, and I ended up in the hospital alone, in the dark, asking God, How did I get here?

In that quiet place, I realized I was never going to be loved right by someone who didn't love themselves. I was never going to be safe with someone who needed me to be small.

I came home different. I ended the relationship. I chose to face whatever was waiting on the other side of that choice, no matter how hard it would be.

🦋 Reflection | Affirmation | Prayer | Action

From Survival to Self-Love

Reflection Questions

1. When you look back, what survival patterns kept you in relationships longer than you should have stayed?
2. How has fear—fear of being alone, fear of starting over—shaped your choices in the past?
3. What moment in your life felt like a "wake-up call" to choose differently?
4. Who do you need to forgive in order to walk forward lighter—yourself included?

Affirmations

- I survived what was meant to destroy me.
- I am no longer defined by what was done to me.
- My awakening is proof of my strength and God's faithfulness.
- I deserve to be free, safe, and whole.

Prayer

Dear Lord,

Thank You for carrying me through seasons I thought would break me. Thank You for protecting me, even when I didn't see it.

Give me the courage to release the pain of my past and the wisdom to see unhealthy patterns clearly.

Help me walk in freedom, with faith that You will provide for me and my children. In Jesus' name, Amen.

Action Step: Naming the Cages

Write down the "cages" you've lived in—

- control
- fear
- shame
- financial dependence
- or anything else.

Then, next to each one, write the truth:

"I am free from this."

Keep it as a reminder that survival is no longer your only story.

Choosing Self-Love and Single Motherhood

Why I Choose Single Motherhood

After all those years, here's what I learned:

- I was already the protector, the provider, the nurturer.
- I was already the one doing everything.
- I was already alone, but with extra burdens.

So, I chose peace. I chose clarity. I chose to rebuild on my own terms.

Single motherhood has been the most peaceful, self-loving thing I have ever done for myself and my children. The freedom to create a life that honors my health, my values, and my dreams has been worth every hard step.

This book is for you if you feel stuck in a life that is breaking your spirit. If you are exhausted by carrying someone else's baggage. If you are ready to choose yourself, even if it means doing it alone.

You are not alone anymore.

I see you.

I am you. And together, we will reclaim our lives.

🦋 Reflection | Affirmation | Prayer | Action

Choosing Self-Love and Single Motherhood

Reflection Questions

1. What lies have you told yourself about what you "deserve" in love and family?
2. What would it mean to choose yourself fully—not halfway, but all the way?
3. How could single motherhood (or simply choosing peace) become an act of self-love for you?
4. What are three things you want to model for your children through your choice?

Affirmations

- I am free to create a life that honors my health, peace, and purpose.
- Choosing myself is not selfish—it is sacred.
- My children are blessed when I am whole.
- Love begins with how I love myself.

Prayer

Father, Thank You for reminding me that I am worthy of love, peace, and joy.

Thank You for giving me the courage to choose myself and my children.

Help me to release fear and step into self-love with boldness.

Guide me as I rebuild a life rooted in faith, freedom, and resilience.

In Jesus' name, Amen.

Action Step: Your Why

Take a few minutes to write down why you are reading this book.

- What are you hoping to find here?
- What are you ready to release?
- What are you ready to build?

Keep this page somewhere safe. This is your first step toward choosing yourself.

Part I: Naming the Truth

Chapter 1: When You're Already the One Doing Everything

For most of my life, I thought I was in relationships. But the truth was simpler—and harder to swallow:

I was alone, with extra work.

When you're the one keeping the bills paid, raising the children, and planning for the future while someone else drains your energy, you are not in a partnership. You are in servitude.

And living with a chronic illness like sickle cell, I really should've been doing less—not so much more.

I remember the exhaustion of trying to get through a flare-up while still caring for everyone else. Cooking, cleaning, teaching, and planning, only to be met with criticism or indifference. Some days, I wondered if I was the problem. If I just tried harder, prayed harder, submitted more, maybe I would finally be loved in return.

But the truth is, no amount of sacrifice can satisfy someone who thrives on your self-betrayal.

Naming this truth is the first step. If you are already doing everything alone, you can choose to do it without the extra burden.

I promise you, Mama—God is all you need. Team up with God until true partners in life are revealed.

A lot of times, we ignore what we see, clinging to the promises we hear. No ma'am—not anymore. From now on, we will listen with our eyes.

- What are the actions saying?
- Are the actions trustworthy?
- Do they match the words, or do they tell a different story?

Stop sitting in lies and stand up in your truth. Once you do, you can start taking steps onto your own path. I can't tell you how long that path will be, but I can say you'll travel lighter without someone constantly complaining and steering you off course.

Most people are drawn to the light you carry.

They'll join you on your journey—until they see what it costs to walk your path.

When they can't keep up, they sabotage and delay.

But that's okay.

That's all they can do.

What's promised to you is yours. All you have to do is get out of your own way and stand up for yourself.

🕊 Reflection | Affirmation | Prayer | Action

When You're Already the One Doing Everything

Reflection Questions

1. What are the things you do every day that no one sees or acknowledges?
2. When you think about your relationship, do you feel supported or drained?
3. What promises have you been holding onto that don't match the reality you're living in?
4. Where have you been ignoring your own needs to avoid conflict?

Affirmation

I am not a burden—I carry more than anyone should.

God sees my strength, and now I do too.

Prayer

God, I've been carrying this weight alone for so long. Help me see what's real. Help me trust what I feel.

Remind me that my needs matter too. Give me the courage to speak up, to step back, to stand firm in your truth and mine.

Walk this path with me. Show me how to travel light. Amen

Action Steps

- Make a list of every responsibility you carry (mental, physical, financial). Seeing it in writing is powerful.
- Journal about how you feel when you imagine doing it all without the extra burden of someone who tears you down.
- Choose one area this week to set a boundary or ask for help—from someone safe, or from God if you don't have help yet.
- Say out loud (or write in a prayer): "I deserve partnership, not servitude. I am allowed to expect better."

Chapter 2: The Myth of Help

People love to say:

"At least you have someone."

"At least you have help."

Let me tell you something:

There is no help in a house where you are the only one showing up.

Help is when someone:

- Takes responsibility
- Shares the weight
- Protects your peace
- Takes tasks off your plate, not adds to them

And if you have a chronic illness, help looks like patience and understanding when you can't carry the normal weight of being a mother and a wife.

Not having the support to handle basic household tasks during a crisis—or help keeping the kids busy while you rest after treatment—hurts in ways people don't see.

Here's something I realized:

People rarely offer help when there's a man standing next to you. They assume you've got support. They don't see that he doesn't clean up after himself and complains more than the kids. They look at you in that situationship and think everything's good: two adults in one household, helping and caring for each other.

I promise you—I've received more help as a single woman than I ever did in a relationship.

Help is not:

- Eating up all your food
- Spending your money
- Draining your spirit
- Driving your car
- Living in your place without financially contributing

In both of my long relationships, I realized too late that the appearance of partnership was just a disguise for control. They used the idea of "help" to keep me small and dependent.

When I finally stopped pretending, it felt like I could breathe for the first time. Seeing things clearly hurt—it stung to accept that I had given years of my life to men who only wanted to tear me down.

Sis, make him show you the steps for the plan. Don't just listen to the words. If you pay close attention, they won't line up.

And the Bible says:

A double-minded man is unstable in all his ways.

The best thing you can do is sit with yourself, look at your real situation, and find a plan that will work for you in the next three months. Build from there.

I promise you—God will help you design a life far better than the lies he's selling you.

🐝 Reflection | Affirmation | Prayer | Action

The Myth of Help

Reflection Questions

1. Who in your life has truly shown up for you without expecting something in return?
2. Have you ever mistaken control for help? What did that cost you?
3. How has chronic illness made it harder for you to ask for or accept real support?
4. What would help look like if it were safe and healthy?

Affirmation

I do not need to prove my worth to be worthy of rest.

I release false help. I receive true support.

Prayer

Lord, I've confused love with labor.

I've welcomed people who didn't value me.

Reveal to me who is for me and who is just near me.

Cut the cords of control and teach me to receive the help you send.

Help me rest in your arms while I rebuild my life with intention. Amen

Action Steps

- Write down what "real help" would look like for you right now—be as specific as you can.
- Practice saying "no" to something small that drains your spirit.
- Identify one person you can trust (a friend, relative, professional) and share honestly about your situation.
- Spend 10 minutes this week creating a backup plan you could lean on if you needed emergency help.

Chapter 3: Chronic Illness as a Catalyst

Managing a chronic illness like sickle cell comes with its own battles. But being with an unsupportive partner? That's one of the worst things you can do to yourself.

Not only will you end up taking on more responsibilities than you should, you also won't get the help you need when it matters most. I remember how my flare-ups were often tied to stress—infidelity, sleepless nights, trying to parent alone, and working full-time.

Having a partner who can't give you peace or rest can literally kill you.

Every time I paused to catch my breath, they acted like I was the laziest person in the world—never seeing all I had already done when they weren't around. I remember homeschooling, cooking, cleaning, managing everything. After the kids finally went outside to play, I sat down for a moment.

Then he walked in. Huffing and puffing. Said something slick like, "You been watching this show all day?" Then stomped out, pretending to be mad. I realized that was his way of escaping to the bar—creating fake arguments to justify leaving.

I used to run myself ragged just trying not to look lazy when he came home. Even then, it turned into,

"You too busy for me."

It took me a long time to understand: These men weren't happy with themselves. Nothing I did could've made them happy with me. I was breaking myself to please people who didn't even value the gift I am.

They took pride in watching me shrink. They felt powerful seeing a queen wait on them hand and foot.

But this queen found her crown.

Living with sickle cell anemia has shaped every decision I've made. Some mornings, I wake up already exhausted. Some days, the pain is so intense I can't even think straight. But the bills don't stop. The kids still need me.

Chronic illness forced me to face a truth I could no longer deny:

If I didn't prioritize my health, nobody else would.

The people I built a life with didn't step in when my body failed. They didn't protect me when I was vulnerable. They used my illness as another way to control me—keeping me dependent, keeping me small.

One of them even said, "You're going to die soon anyway."

That hit hard. My sister passed from the same disease, so those words were cruel. Insensitive. And the worst part? He said that to the same woman who birthed and cares for his kids.

Yes, I have sickle cell. And yes, one day I will die.

But let's be real—none of us gets out of here alive.

At least now I walk with my head held high. In peace. In freedom. Knowing I'm living a better life—for me.

And you know what? That same illness set me free.

Because when you're fighting to survive, you stop tolerating what drains you.

In the silence of a hospital room, I came face-to-face with my truth—and I stood in it.

I would rather be alone in my sickness than alone in a relationship pretending to be loved.

Since ending that relationship, I've lost weight. I experience fewer flare-ups. Sickle cell will do what it does—but I'll be damned if I let toxic people make it worse.

🦋 Reflection | Prayer | Affirmation | Action

Chronic Illness as a Catalyst

Reflection Questions

1. In what ways has your illness forced you to face the truth about your relationships?
2. How have you allowed stress and toxic dynamics to impact your health?
3. When was the last time you felt truly peaceful in your own home?
4. If you believed you deserved to be protected and cherished, what decisions would you make?

Affirmation

My illness does not make me weak.

My boundaries do not make me selfish.

I protect my peace because I matter.

Prayer

God, you know the pain I carry in my bones and in my heart.

Thank you for staying with me when others left.

Give me the strength to heal, even while I hurt.

Teach me to say no without guilt and to say yes to the life you've prepared for me.

Let my healing begin with truth and end with peace.

Action Steps

- Make a list of everything you do to care for your health. Circle the things you could do more consistently if you weren't carrying other people's baggage.
- Write a letter to yourself acknowledging all you've survived. Keep it somewhere you can read it on hard days.
- Commit to removing or reducing one source of unnecessary stress over the next month.
- Each morning this week, repeat: "I will not let anyone make my illness worse. I protect my peace because my life matters."

Chapter 4: The Moment You Decide: No More Pretending

There is always a moment.

For some women, it's quiet—a thought that slips in late at night:

I can't do this anymore.

For me, it was the day I was in the hospital after my health broke down again. I was lying there, wondering if I was going to die. And I knew:

If I was going to be alone in the dark, I would rather be alone in the light, too.

I remember one of the few times he came to visit during that serious health crisis. He sat in the chair beside me, staring at boats on his phone. Not long after, he bought a boat—with the last of our money—while I was fighting for my life.

Meanwhile, the kids were calling me, asking if I could DoorDash them dinner because they hadn't eaten. I was hooked up to oxygen and IVs while he was out on dates, eating good, and running up my credit cards.

I had a very long conversation with God that day. I asked Him to make a way home to my kids—a way out of this mess. And then it hit me like a bus:

If I die here today, who will care for my children?

Who would look after them if their dad—my so-called partner—had already checked out?

I had carried the weight of this family for years, but in that moment, I finally saw why I shouldn't.

Not only did it cost me my health—almost my life—it was going to cost my children so much more.

I used to think I was managing his drama and stupidity by ignoring him and just doing everything myself. But what happens when I'm gone? He never grew into a man who could take care of me or this household. How was he going to take care of the kids and do what I did?

The truth was, he couldn't.

In trying to save everybody and do everything, I was crippling my own home. I was halfway in and halfway out. I knew the right answers, but I was letting someone undermine me.

I was trying to be a wife who listens and follows. But what do you do when he's talking foolishness and leading you down a path to nowhere?

Here's what I learned: When you're trying to be a good woman to a bad man, you will always lose.

And God said to me, You already know what needs to be done if you want to live—and if you want your kids to have a chance to win at life.

I came home different.

I stopped explaining.

I stopped asking for permission to save myself.

That's what this book is about:

Naming the truth so you can build a life based on it.

🕊 Reflection | Affirmation | Prayer | Action

When you stop pretending, you can start rebuilding

Reflection Questions

1. In what ways have you been carrying everything alone?
2. What "help" have you been telling yourself you have—even when you know it isn't real?
3. How has your health—mental or physical—forced you to confront the truth about your situation?
4. What moment stands out as the time you knew you had to change something?

Affirmation

"I no longer carry illusions. I see the truth clearly, and I choose to live in it. Pretending ends today, and rebuilding begins now."

Prayer

Lord, open my eyes to the truth of my situation.

Remove the blinders of fear, denial, and false hope. Give me the courage to stop pretending, the wisdom to see what is real, and the strength to act on what You reveal.

Let my honesty be the foundation of my healing and my children's future. Amen.

Action Step: Naming Your Truth

Write down one sentence that describes your reality as honestly as possible.

No sugarcoating. No excuses.

Examples:

- I am carrying this household alone.
- I am pretending to be in a relationship that doesn't exist.
- I am staying because I'm afraid of starting over.

Keep this sentence visible—in your journal, on a sticky note, or somewhere private. Let it be your line in the sand: the truth you will no longer deny.

Part II: Reclaiming Your Life

Chapter 5: Housing as Freedom

One of the most important things I ever did was find my own place to live.

When I picked my house, I knew exactly what it would become. He called it a trap house. He couldn't see past the broken mess, couldn't see the potential. But I did.

I knew this house would be a place for my kids to grow up and thrive. I knew I'd make it a home—full of stability and peace.

In my first relationship, he would put me out constantly. I remember sleeping in the laundry room in the basement of our apartment building. I almost got assaulted at the park one night, trying to sleep on a bench. But I was a fighter.

In my next relationship, I finally had a house that was mine on paper. But his presence and energy were so massive and toxic, it turned my home into a prison. He slammed doors and drawers. Threw unpredictable tantrums. Stayed out all night. Just pure bullying.

After years of feeling trapped in someone else's space—someone else's rules, moods, and chaos—

having my own key felt like finally being able to breathe.

The first time I experienced this freedom was when I left the first man. It wasn't fancy. I didn't have all the furniture. I traded food stamps for a used couch and accepted hand-me-downs from neighbors. But it was mine.

The second time was when I finally got my second not-husband out of the house. It took almost a year of him living in the basement apartment, playing games—moving out and then moving back in. I planned to evict him formally, but eventually, he got the hint and left.

Housing is more than shelter.

It's a boundary.

It is a declaration:

This is my space.

This is my peace.

This is where you can start to heal by creating an environment that belongs only to you.

If you are thinking about leaving or have already left, here are truths to hold onto:

- You don't have to wait until you can afford the perfect place.
- Safe and stable is more important than big or beautiful.
- Even a small corner of your own can change your life.

When I signed that lease without anyone else's name on it, it was the first time I felt truly free.

No one could threaten to kick me out.

No one could withhold a key. I wasn't trapped anymore.

🕊 Reflection | Affirmation | Prayer | Action

Housing as Freedom

Your space is your sanctuary

Reflection Questions

1. What does "home" mean to you when you imagine it without fear or chaos?
2. Have you ever felt trapped in someone else's space or energy? What did that do to your spirit?
3. What small steps could you take to create a peaceful environment—whether it's a whole house or just a room?
4. What fears come up when you think about having your own place?

Affirmation

"My home is my sanctuary. I deserve safety, peace, and stability in the place where I live."

Prayer

Lord, thank You for the gift of shelter. I ask You to protect my home and make it a place of peace.

Give me wisdom as I make decisions about where to live and courage to claim space that is mine.

Help me to build an environment where my children and I can heal, grow, and thrive. Amen.

Action Step: Creating a Vision

Write one sentence that describes the home you want to build—emotionally and physically.

Examples:

- My home will be a place of peace and rest.
- I will never again let anyone make me feel unsafe where I live.
- I deserve to have a space that is mine alone.

Keep this sentence somewhere you can see it often as you take steps toward your freedom.

Chapter 6: Financial Foundations

Leaving a toxic relationship without a plan for money can feel terrifying.

That's why so many women stay.

I know—because I was there.

In my first relationship, he took most of my paycheck and controlled every bill. He made sure I couldn't afford to leave.

In my second, he told me that any money left after the bills was "his." Like I was a guest in my own life.

Let me tell you something:

I don't care what kind of money he's making or what kind of life he's promising you.

Go find yourself a safe place to live, and go run up a check.

Trust me—I left a man who was making really good money. But it doesn't matter how much he earns if you can't control any of it—or if he can't control himself.

Think about it:

With all the money he brings into the house, how much goes to you and your needs? How much goes to the kids? How much goes to expenses you never agreed to?

And how much do you contribute?

Now ask yourself the question most women are too afraid to face:

Can you do it on your own?

It's not about whether you want to—it's about whether you could.

If he died tomorrow, could you keep going?

Sometimes it's not a breakup. Sometimes it could be death.

You are doing yourself a disservice by not being stable on your own. When you build that stability, you'll have more freedom and power to make better decisions.

Money is a powerful tool.

I learned this, and by the grace of God, I've learned a lot over the years about budgeting on a low income.

I'm a mom, so we just inherit the skill of figuring it out.

And I'm not too proud to go without so my children can have what they need.

You will have to sacrifice superficial stuff to have the money for what matters.

But the reward of financial freedom will be priceless.

Breaking the Pattern

Breaking that pattern meant doing three things:

1. Learning the Numbers

- How much I earned, exactly.
- How much the bills were.
- What I could cut back or eliminate.

2. Opening My Own Accounts

- A bank account in only my name.
- A secret emergency fund.
- Cash savings if I couldn't trust the bank.

3. Making an Exit Budget

- One month of rent and bills set aside.
- Groceries and essentials for my kids.

- Enough to keep the lights on while I caught my breath.

It wasn't perfect or quick.

But over time, those steps gave me options.

If you are afraid to look at the numbers, remember:

No reality is scarier than staying stuck.

Start small—and remember: sometimes all you need is enough for bus fare to get away.

🕊 Reflection | Affirmation | Prayer | Action

Financial Foundations

Money is freedom, not fear

Reflection Questions

1. What beliefs about money have kept you tied to unhealthy situations?
2. What would financial freedom mean for you and your children?
3. What small steps can you take this week to start separating your finances?
4. What is one thing you could go without temporarily to save money for your exit plan?

Affirmation

"I am capable of providing for myself and my children. My financial stability is a tool for freedom, not fear."

Prayer

Father, thank You for being my ultimate Provider.

Teach me how to be a wise steward of my money.

Break every chain of fear, lack, or dependence that has kept me tied to unhealthy situations.

Help me to create financial order, so I can walk in the freedom You designed for me. Amen.

Action Step: Know Your Numbers

1. Write down exactly how much money comes in, how much goes out, and how much you control.
2. Then, list one thing you can do this month to start building financial independence.

Examples:

- Open a personal checking account.
- Start a cash envelope with just $20.
- Make a list of expenses to reduce or eliminate.

Keep this list somewhere private but visible to remind you: You are capable of providing for yourself.

Chapter 7: Legal and Practical Protections

I remember when my ex and I split up.

The only thing that stayed together after that relationship was the debt we'd accumulated—well over $100,000 total. Credit cards, unsecured loans, car payments, the mortgage, bills, and of course, the children—yeah, all that stayed with me.

Why? Because he was the income, and I was the credit. My name was on everything. Even though he used the authorized cards linked to my account, and the loans were for home repairs and remodels, the debt was all in my name. With trust and a promise to pay, I ended up holding the bag.

And with my health issues, I'm now on a fixed income. So, those monthly payments bankrupted me. I had no financial recourse. We weren't married, and we didn't have anything in writing.

So let me be clear:

Do not put your name on anything unless it's truly yours and you're sure you can pay for it yourself.

After a breakup or divorce, if it's not court-ordered, remove them from your accounts and close any shared credit cards. My ex was still on my bank account and kept over drafting it, eventually causing the account to be closed. I ended up having to pay his balance of over $500 because I was the primary account holder.

People rarely talk about the legal side of reclaiming your life, but it matters.

When you share children, property, or debt with someone, you need to protect yourself.

Here are some steps that helped me (and might help you):

Custody and Visitation

- Get your parenting time in writing.
- Know your rights—even if you were never legally married.
- Document everything.

After the relationship ended, promises about visitation and financial help were made but never kept.

If you're making arrangements outside the court system, put them in writing so you have something to refer back to in court if needed.

Medical Directives and Guardianship

- If you have a chronic illness, decide who will care for your kids if you are hospitalized.
- Complete paperwork that names a trusted adult—not your ex—who can make decisions if you can't.

Housing Protections

- Whenever possible, put your lease or mortgage only in your name.
- Keep proof of your payments and agreements.

Never put his name on anything. He should have his own. Or, if he wants to contribute, let him buy something you both share after marriage.

But anything before marriage—oh no, sis, get your paperwork right. You worked too hard to let someone have access to something they didn't earn.

Financial Separation

- Remove your name from joint accounts and loans.
- Change all your passwords and PINs.
- Set up direct deposit into an account only you control.

It can feel overwhelming, but every small action you take makes you safer and freer.

🦋 Reflection | Affirmation | Prayer | Action

Legal and Practical Protections

Protect what's yours

Reflection Questions

1. What legal or financial ties are still connecting you to someone who no longer supports you?
2. What boundaries do you need to set around your housing, money, or children?
3. Who can you trust to help you understand your rights and options?
4. How would it feel to know your life, home, and finances were truly secure?

Affirmation

"I am not powerless. I can protect myself, my children, and everything God has entrusted to me."

Prayer

Lord, give me clarity and courage as I take practical steps to protect myself and my children.

Remove confusion and fear, and place trustworthy people in my life who can guide me through the legal and financial details.

Cover my home, my money, and my children with Your protection. Amen.

Action Step: Make Your First Move

Pick one thing from this list to do this week:

- Gather and copy your important documents (ID, birth certificates, leases).
- Open a bank account in only your name.
- Start a written list of all your bills and their amounts.
- Research rental options, even if you're not ready to move yet.

You don't have to do everything at once. One step is enough to start.

Part III: Healing from the Past

Chapter 8: Grieving What You Thought You Had

People assume that when you leave a bad relationship, all you feel is relief. But the truth is more complicated. I had to grieve the life I thought I was building.

The story I told myself about who we were and what we could become. Even when the reality was toxic, the dream was still beautiful.

I knew who he was before I committed to him. But I was committed to the man he could become—not who he really was.

I could tell he was lost and searching, and I tried to give him space to grow and understanding to change. But when you're that lost, you can seek guidance from the wrong people. When you should be seeking guidance from God.

That's why it's so important to know your own wants and needs before entering into any relationship. If you don't, your heart and hopes will breathe life into a beautiful fantasy that turns into a living nightmare.

I had to heal from something that should have been beautiful. Here we were—this Black family, two working parents, homeschooling, homeowners remodeling with all new furniture and appliances, most gifted from my father.

New model luxury cars. On our way to a six-figure income. Setting a standard for our children and daughters, breaking generational curses. And then—suddenly—we became another statistic.

Baby mama, baby daddy drama. No thank you. I opt out. But, I do stand in my truth and am committed to become what I know I am. Always have and always will be, to my dying breath: A mother.

And of course, I grieved the idea of partnership.

I'm also just a girl. He cheated on me and called me names. Yall He hurt my feelings in real life. I only risked my life to bring forth his children.

But the hardest part to bury was the hope. The hope that one day he would finally see me. That he would wake up and realize I was worth protecting. Worth loving right.

When you leave, you are not just walking away from a person. You are burying a future that never came. Grief doesn't mean you made the wrong decision. It means you are finally honest about what was never there.

🦋 Reflection | Prayer | Affirmation | Action

Grieving What You Thought You Had

Reflection Questions

1. What dreams or visions did you hold onto in this relationship, even when reality didn't match?
2. In what ways did you abandon your own needs or voice to preserve the fantasy?
3. What does it mean to you to grieve something you never really had?
4. What parts of that vision were worth honoring, even if the relationship failed?

Affirmations

I honor the love I tried to build, even if it wasn't returned.

My grief is proof that I loved with my whole heart.

I release the fantasy that kept me stuck.

I am worthy of real, healthy, lasting love.

I am enough, exactly as I am.

A Prayer for Healing Grief

Dear God, Help me lay to rest the future I dreamed of but never received. Comfort me as I grieve not just what I lost, but what never was.

Teach me to forgive myself for believing in potential instead of reality.

Restore my hope and remind me that Your plans for me are better than any fantasy I could imagine. Amen.

Action Step

- Take 15 minutes to write a goodbye letter to the version of the relationship you thought you had.
- Say everything you never said.
- When you finish, destroy or safely burn the letter as a symbol of release.

Chapter 9: Releasing Guilt and Shame

If you've ever stayed longer than you should have, you know this feeling:

- What is wrong with me?
- Why didn't I leave sooner?

I asked myself those same questions—over and over again. But here's what I learned:

- You don't owe anyone an explanation for surviving the best way you knew how.
- You stayed because you were taught to put everyone else first.
- You stayed because you were scared.
- You stayed because you believed in hope.

That doesn't make you weak. That makes you human.

1. Shame keeps you silent.
2. Guilt keeps you stuck.

The only way to release them is to tell the truth—even when it shakes you to your core:

"I did the best I could with what I had." And that is enough. You are enough.

Silly Girl

We all have seasons in life where we find ourselves somewhere we don't want to be because we were being dumb.

I call it the "Stupid Season."

The time when you're so caught up doing the wrong thing, for the wrong reasons, with the wrong people—you can't even see straight.

You're spinning in a cyclone of chaos, making bad decisions on top of bad decisions.

And then—suddenly—you get spit out.

You're laying there, looking back at the storm you barely survived, finally able to see the damage... and the truth.

The person you see in those memories was hurt.

Broken.

Used.

But you?

You are still here.

Bruised, banged up, but standing.

You get up.

You dust yourself off.

And you walk in the opposite direction.

We don't have to go chasing storms—life will send them on its own.

But we do have to rebuild.

We have to prepare for the next season. The next storm.

Because your life will have storms.

But as you learn and grow, your tools get stronger.

Your foundation gets wiser.

Give yourself grace.

Keep going.

This too shall pass.

It's just a season.

🦋 Reflection | Prayer | Affirmation | Action

Releasing Guilt and Shame

Reflection Questions

1. What beliefs or fears kept you in a place that wasn't safe for your soul?
2. How do guilt and shame show up in your body, your thoughts, or your voice?
3. What would it feel like to forgive the version of you that stayed too long?
4. What does your "storm survival story" teach you about your strength?

Affirmations

- I release the guilt that does not belong to me.
- I forgive myself for what I didn't know back then.
- My story is full of lessons, not shame.
- I am not defined by my past—I am empowered by what I've overcome.
- I honor the woman I was and celebrate the woman I am becoming.

A Healing Prayer

God, I carry shame and guilt like bricks on my back.

But I know You didn't design me to live this way.

Help me lay it all down—at Your feet.

Remind me that I was doing the best I could.

Heal the parts of me that still feel stuck in the storm.

And show me how to walk forward in freedom.
Amen.

Action Step

- Write a letter to your "Stupid Season" self.
- Speak to her with grace, not judgment.
- Thank her for surviving.

Let her know she doesn't have to carry the shame anymore. Burn or rip the letter as a sign of release.

Chapter 10: Rebuilding Your Identity

When you've spent years being someone's caretaker, someone's emotional punching bag, or someone's shadow, you forget who you are.

For a long time, I didn't know what I liked.

What I believed.

What I wanted.

Everything in my life had been shaped around other people's needs.

For the first time, I was able to think of my own needs—and there's no lie in that statement.

Healing meant learning to ask myself simple questions:

1. What makes me feel peaceful?
2. What do I believe about love?
3. What does success look like for me—not for anyone else?

I had to rebuild my identity from scratch.

Piece by piece, I started to remember who I was before the world told me I was only valuable when I was useful to others.

Being a single but in-a-relationship mom with sickle cell was difficult. But somehow, being a single mom with sickle cell feels simpler.

Before, my days were chaotic and draining. Now, they are slow and peaceful. Stress still comes, but I handle it so much better because I am the head of my household. And when I can't figure it out, I go to God.

Speaking of God—I've been able to find my faith again.

It had been so warped by that relationship that we stopped having faith in our savior.

I was trying to follow a man without faith, while raising my children with faith— also trying to teach them faith without Christ—was confusing.

Being so conflicted inside was eating my soul from the inside out. When I left, I thought I'd feel lost forever.

And I did feel lost for some years. Although I'm still a work in progress and I don't know all the things about my new state of self-being.

But I do know this:

I am a child of God.

I know who I am because I know whose I am.

And that's on Mr. Golden.

I can do all things through Christ who strengthens me.

Don't worry too much about who you are right now.

Go find out who God is.

Through the work and the seeking, you will discover who you are.

Talk to God.

Talk to yourself.

Journal, speak, pray, write.

Get it all out.

Get to know yourself all over again—

you've changed.

🦋 Reflection | Prayer | Affirmation | Action

Rebuilding Your Identity

Reflection Questions

1. In what ways did you shape your life around other people's expectations?
2. What parts of yourself are you now rediscovering or reclaiming?
3. How has reconnecting with faith changed your sense of identity?
4. What does "peace" look like in this season of your life?

Affirmations

I am allowed to redefine who I am at any time.

My worth is not measured by what I do for others.

I am a child of God, and I am loved beyond measure.

Each day, I become more of the woman I was created to be.

I honor my growth, even when it feels slow.

Prayer

Dear God,

Thank You for reminding me who I am.

When I feel lost, help me remember that I am never beyond Your reach.

Teach me to see myself the way You see me—whole, worthy, loved.

Guide me as I rebuild my identity rooted in You. Amen.

Action Step

- Set aside 20 minutes to journal about this question:

"Who am I becoming?"

- Write without editing or judging. Let your spirit speak freely.

Chapter 11: Reconnecting with God and Your Spirit

In my darkest moments, I realized I had been looking to men to give me something only God could.

- Approval.
- Worth.
- A sense of belonging.

See, I was raised to be a good Apostolic girl. My closest friends were Baptist, and I went to church with them a lot. I loved it.

I'm still not sure how I went from that to nothing at all.

I always had faith, but somewhere along the way, we removed everything that seemed religious or spiritual. Christian. Any of it.

Why did I do that?

Repeat after me:

"I was in my stupid season. Don't talk about me—pray for me."

The Holy Spirit will speak to you.

Then it'll get louder.

Then it will nudge you.

Then tap you on the shoulder.

Then it will shake you.

Slap you.

And eventually, it will go tell God in you.

Now you're getting an epic ass whooping from your Heavenly Father. And you're wishing you had listened to that feeling you had in the beginning.

But things happen for a reason, and all things are according to God's timing.

Let's not get it twisted, though—

You were being stupid.

But in God's favor, He brought you out and opened your eyes.

Otherwise, you wouldn't be here reading this book.

No matter what you've been through—no matter how bad it seemed—

God has a plan.

And ALL THINGS WORK.

Leaving those relationships brought me back to the quiet places where I could hear God again.

I didn't have all the answers.

I still don't.

But I started praying for strength instead of solutions.

For peace instead of perfection.

I'm humbling myself daily to yield my life to the Creator. Sometimes God puts you alone so you and Him can have some alone time. It's not always a bad thing. God is cool to talk to—No judgment, just a listening ear.

If you want something, just ask. But be open to the delivery, because God is a clever being.

Blessings might be staring you in the face—They're just packaged differently than you expect.

If you are feeling alone in this journey, know this:

You are never alone.

God has never left you.

And you are worthy of love, just as you are.

🐝 Reflection | Prayer | Affirmation | Action

Reconnecting with God and Your Spirit

Reflection Questions

1. Where in your life have you been trying to get from people what only God can give?
2. What parts of your faith have you abandoned, and why?
3. What would it look like to invite God back into your daily life?
4. What blessings might be in front of you right now, disguised as something else?

Affirmations

I am never alone—God is always with me.

My worth comes from my Creator, not from anyone else.

I am loved exactly as I am.

Even in my mistakes, God's grace covers me.

I am open to hearing God's voice and receiving His blessings.

Healing Prayer

Dear God, Thank You for never giving up on me.

Thank You for finding me in my stupid season and loving me anyway.

Help me release the shame I've carried about turning away from You.

Show me how to trust You again and walk in faith every day.

Fill my heart with Your peace and my spirit with Your strength. Amen.

Action Step

Create a "Faith List."

Write down three simple ways you can reconnect with God this week.

Examples:

- Spend five minutes in quiet prayer each morning
- Read one Bible verse a day
- Write a gratitude list and thank God for each item

Choose one to start today.

Part IV: Thriving as a Single Mother by Choice

Chapter 12: Redefining Success on Your Terms

When I finally stood on my own, I realized that most of what I thought I wanted wasn't even mine.

I had spent years measuring my life against other people's expectations of what a "good girl" looked like.

Even though we weren't married on paper, I still took all my roles seriously. I was doing all the things to create a picture-perfect life—something to be proud of.

Meanwhile, the person beside me kept saying it wasn't enough.

His constant wanting had me thinking we needed more and more.

So, we worked and worked for things society told us we needed.

We pretended to be what the world told us to be.

- You should be married by now.
- You should have a two-parent household.

- You should do whatever it takes to keep your family together.

But none of those voices were God's voice.

None of them came from that quiet knowing in my own heart.

Thriving means defining success for yourself.

When I finally stood in my truth, I realized:

God had already blessed me with everything I needed.

I've always been a chill chick. A homebody, if you will.

I consider myself practical and low-maintenance—some might say too low-maintenance, but that's okay.

People may see me as poor.

But through Christ, I'm rich in ways the eye can't measure.

I've learned to appreciate the things money can't buy—

and use money to enhance those things, not replace them.

For me, success looks like:

- A home that feels peaceful, even when it's imperfect
- Children who know they are safe and loved
- A life that honors my health and energy
- Enough flexibility to rest when my body demands it

When you stop living by someone else's standards, you finally get to decide what thriving feels like.

🦋 Reflection | Prayer | Affirmation | Action

Redefining Success on Your Terms

Reflection Questions

1. Where did your old definition of "success" come from? Who planted those seeds?
2. What does success look like in your season of life right now?
3. How does honoring your energy and needs shift your goals?
4. Are there parts of your current life that already reflect success—but you haven't celebrated them yet?

Affirmations

I get to define success on my terms.

I am already living in blessings others can't see.

My worth is not measured by status or comparison.

I honor a life that matches my truth, not the world's expectations.

I have everything I need for this moment, and more is coming.

A Prayer for Freedom from Comparison

Dear God, Thank You for giving me a purpose that doesn't depend on the world's approval.

Help me release every lie I've believed about what success should look like.

Open my eyes to the beauty of my current blessings.

Remind me that a peaceful life is a prosperous life.

Help me walk boldly in my own lane—with joy, rest, and gratitude. Amen.

Action Step

- Make a new "Success List" based on your values.
- Write down 5 things that represent success for your life—right now.
- Place the list somewhere visible as a daily reminder that your lane is enough.

Chapter 13: Building a Home That Heals

After years of chaos and conflict, I knew my home had to be different.

I wanted it to be a sanctuary—not just a place to sleep.

That meant:

- Creating routines that worked for us, not for appearances
- Decluttering anything that carried memories of pain
- Filling my walls with words and images that reminded me of hope
- Teaching my children that home is a soft place to land

You don't need expensive things to create a healing space.

- You need intention.
- You need love.
- You need the courage to protect your peace.

The trick isn't to be extreme.

It's to be you.

For me, building my place of peace meant looking past the bad memories in my home and creating new ones.

I went through a season of rage where I purged everything—painting the walls, throwing away broken things, decluttering every corner.

Creating peace in a home you once shared with someone is hard.

But being homeless is harder.

I take my blessings wherever I can find them.

The key is finding peace and stillness in the present—while holding active faith for the future.

This is just another season.

Maybe a ghetto season.

But we all have them.

They build character.

I promise you:

You already have everything you need right now.

And if you feel you don't—work with what you've got.

Be patient.

More will come.

Create the joy.

Create the comfort.

Even if it's just a corner.

My home is my healing place.

I've created different areas to focus on different things:

- A place to work and decompress between daily life
- A space outside to relax and touch grass

Having my own house means I get to do yard work. And though it can be hard or painful at times, nothing cures mental stress quite like a hard day's work—especially in the sun.

You realize you have a lot to be grateful for.

🕊 Reflection | Prayer | Affirmation | Action

Building a Home That Heals

Reflection Questions

1. What does "home" mean to you at this season of your life?
2. What parts of your space still hold memories or energy you need to release?
3. How can you create comfort and peace with what you already have?
4. What small corner or ritual could become your sanctuary?

Affirmations

My home is a safe place for my spirit to rest.

I release the past and make room for new memories.

I am worthy of peace and beauty in my surroundings.

I can create healing spaces, no matter my circumstances.

Gratitude fills every room in my home.

A Healing Prayer

Dear God, Thank You for giving me this space to rebuild and begin again.

Help me release any heaviness lingering in these walls.

Fill every corner with Your peace, Your love, and Your protection.

Teach me to see my home as a blessing, even in its imperfections.

May this place be a refuge for me and my children. Amen.

Action Step

Create One Healing Corner.

Pick one spot—a chair, a corner of your bedroom, or a porch—and make it your sanctuary.

Add something comforting:

- A soft blanket
- A candle
- A favorite book
- A plant or fresh flowers

Spend a few minutes there each day to ground and refresh yourself.

Chapter 14: Raising Whole, Resilient Children

One of the lies people love to tell single mothers is that your children will be broken because you left.

But here is what I know:

Children are not harmed by the absence of a marriage certificate.

They are harmed by the presence of chaos, neglect, and disrespect.

Your children are watching you:

- Choose peace over pretending
- Tell the truth even when it costs you
- Love yourself enough to walk away

That is a gift they will carry forever.

I don't pretend it's easy.

Some days, I feel guilt that I couldn't give my kids a "traditional" family.

But I remind myself:

- I am giving them something better—safety, honesty, and freedom.
- I'm teaching them that love is not something you have to earn by shrinking yourself.
- I'm showing them that their needs matter, and so do mine.
- I'm proving that you can rebuild after loss—and still be whole.

Our children don't need us to be perfect. They need us to be present, real, and willing to grow alongside them.

When you heal, your children feel it.

When you stand up for yourself, they learn to stand up for themselves.

That is legacy.

That is breaking cycles.

That is love in action.

🦋 Reflection | Affirmation | Prayer | Action

Raising Whole, Resilient Children

Reflection Questions

1. What values do you want your children to see you living out every day?
2. How do you show your children that they are safe and loved?
3. What family traditions or routines bring you connection and joy?
4. What old beliefs about single motherhood are you ready to release?

Affirmations

- My children are blessed, whole, and deeply loved.
- I am enough as I am.
- Our family is strong because we are honest and safe together.
- I am building a new legacy, one choice at a time.
- My love is the foundation my children will always stand on.

Prayer

Dear God, Thank You for the precious souls You've entrusted to my care.

Cover my children with Your protection and peace.

Help me guide them with wisdom and grace.

Fill our home with laughter, safety, and unconditional love.

Teach them to see their worth through Your eyes and mine.

Amen.

Action Step: Legacy in Practice

Choose one value you want to model for your children this week (e.g., honesty, kindness, resilience).

Be intentional in showing it—then tell your children why it matters. This builds legacy through daily actions.

Chapter 15: Moms Raising Daughters

As a mother who has lived through both hardship and hope, I understand my role as a container of wisdom meant to be poured into my children.

My daughters will one day navigate this world on their own, and if all I can do is tell them my story and equip them with tools I never had, they will be better off than I was.

Here are a few of the things I intentionally teach my daughters about financial independence and self-reliance—lessons I believe every young woman deserves to know:

1. The Importance of Financial Independence

    No one should rely on another person for their entire financial well-being. True strength comes from being able to stand on your own two feet.

2. Budgeting and Saving

    Track income, manage expenses, and prioritize saving—even if it's small.

Emergency funds and long-term goals create freedom.

3. Understanding Credit and Debt

   Debt can become a trap. Credit should be used wisely, not as a crutch. Good credit is valuable, but peace of mind is worth more.

4. Setting Financial Goals

   Whether it's a car, college, or retirement, goal-setting teaches focus and intentional living.

5. Investing Wisely

   The earlier, the better. Compound interest, property, and education are all assets that multiply.

6. Self-Worth and Financial Boundaries

   Their worth is never tied to who pays the bills. Relationships should never come with financial manipulation or control.

7. Recognizing Red Flags in Relationships

   A partner who is irresponsible, manipulative, or lazy will cost you more than money. Values matter more than vibes.

8. Negotiating Salaries and Raises

   They must know their worth and never be afraid to advocate for themselves.

9. Owning Assets, Not Liabilities

   Cars depreciate, homes appreciate. Choose wisely what you put your money into.

10. Confidence in Financial Decision-Making

Trusting their instincts and knowledge will keep them from being swayed by poor advice or unhealthy dependency.

By empowering my daughters with this knowledge, I am helping them walk into adulthood equipped, confident, and free.

My hope is that they will never stay where they are not valued—financially, emotionally, or spiritually.

🦋 Reflection | Affirmation | Prayer | Action

Moms Raising Daughters

Reflection Questions

1. What lessons about money, independence, or boundaries do you wish someone had taught you earlier?
2. How can you model financial wisdom and confidence for your daughters in daily life?
3. What fears or doubts do you carry about your daughters' future, and how can you replace them with faith and preparation?
4. How do you want your daughters to remember your guidance when they face challenges of their own?

Affirmations

My daughters are strong, wise, and capable of making their own way.

I am equipping them with the tools I never had.

My story is not a burden—it is a blueprint of resilience.

I raise my daughters to value themselves and their independence.

Through faith, love, and wisdom, I am breaking generational cycles.

Prayer

Dear Lord, Thank You for the gift of my daughters.

Help me to pour wisdom into them with patience and love.

Teach me to guide them without fear, and to prepare them without control.

Cover them with protection as they grow into women of strength and character.

Let them always know their worth—through Your eyes and mine. Amen.

Action Step: Passing the Torch

- Choose one financial or life principle from this chapter that you want your daughters to remember.
- Share it with them in a simple, practical way this week—through a conversation, a story, or a small activity.
- Write it down together so it becomes part of their toolkit for the future.

Chapter 16: Moms Raising Sons

Raising my son comes with unique joys and challenges.

While many of the lessons I teach my daughters—such as integrity, responsibility, and financial wisdom—also apply to him, there are aspects of his role in life as a potential husband, father, and protector that require intentional teaching.

I want him to grow into a man who treats, protects, and provides for all the women in his life with respect, care, and humility. Life will be complicated, messy, and sometimes confusing, but through God's guidance, he can learn to do what is right—even when it's hard.

There's a saying that a woman can't raise a man. While some may debate this, I believe I can raise a boy to be more Christlike. I may not know every challenge he will face, but I can instill in him the principles and precepts of the Bible, and I can model Christlike behavior through my own life.

To support this, I created a "WWJD" (What Would Jesus Do?) homeschool curriculums for all my children, with special focus on my son.

Through scripture, examples, and discussion, he learns about character, courage, service, and love—the blueprint for becoming the kind of man Jesus modeled.

All I can do is teach him what is right, provide clear examples, and trust God with the rest.

Practical Lessons for Raising Sons

1. Integrity and Honesty

    His word is his bond. Being truthful, even when it's hard, builds trust and respect.

2. Respect for Women

    He must honor, protect, and value women in his life—mother, sisters, friends, and future partner.

3. Financial Responsibility

    Budgeting, saving, and making wise spending choices are key. Understanding credit, debt, and building assets prepares him for independence.

4. Work Ethic and Discipline

    Success requires effort, focus, and consistency. Responsibility for his actions and goals is essential.

5. Emotional Intelligence

   He should identify, process, and express emotions in healthy ways. Feeling and speaking his truth is strength.

6. Faith and Spiritual Growth

   Daily prayer, scripture reading, and reflection teach that wisdom and strength come from God.

7. Problem-Solving and Critical Thinking

   Challenges are opportunities to think, create, and seek guidance thoughtfully.

8. Leadership and Service

   Lead by example, serve others, and care for those around him.

9. Self-Worth and Boundaries

   His value is not determined by others' opinions. Healthy boundaries are essential in relationships and friendships.

10. Courage and Resilience

    Failures and setbacks are part of life. Facing them with courage and learning from mistakes builds character.

Reflection | Affirmation | Prayer | Action

Moms Raising Sons

Reflection Questions

1. Which qualities do I most want my son to embody as a man of faith and integrity?
2. How can I model Christlike behavior for him in my daily actions?
3. Which challenges in his future can I help prepare him for through practical lessons and spiritual guidance?
4. How can I teach him to honor and respect women while developing independence and resilience?

Affirmations

My son is strong, compassionate, and guided by faith.

I am equipping him to make wise, Christ-centered choices.

My teaching and example give him a blueprint for godly manhood.

Through love, patience, and scripture, I help him grow into a man of character.

I trust God to guide his heart, mind, and actions.

Prayer

Dear Lord, Thank You for the gift of my son.

Help me to guide him with wisdom, patience, and love.

Teach me to model the life of Christ so he can see integrity, courage, and compassion in action.

Protect him as he grows, and help him to honor You in every decision he makes.

May he become a man who uplifts others, respects women, and follows Your ways. Amen.

Action Step: Building a Godly Man

- Choose one lesson from this chapter—such as integrity, respect, or resilience—that you want your son to embrace.
- Create a small activity, conversation, or real-life scenario this week to demonstrate it.
- Write down a verse or story together that illustrates this principle and place it somewhere visible to remind him daily.

Chapter 17: Cultivating Joy and Purpose

Thriving isn't just about getting by—

It's about allowing yourself to feel joy again.

For a long time, I was too tired, too sick, and too drained to even imagine what happiness could look like.

But over time, I started to find little sparks:

- A quiet morning coffee before the kids woke up
- A walk outside on a day when my pain was manageable
- A project or dream that had nothing to do with anyone else's expectations

Joy doesn't have to be big.

It doesn't have to be loud.

It just has to be yours.

And purpose is what keeps you going.

For me, purpose became telling the truth, helping other mothers, and trusting that God didn't bring me through all this for nothing.

Maybe you don't know exactly what your purpose looks like yet. That's okay.

Start by noticing what makes your spirit feel alive.

Pay attention to the moments when you forget to be afraid.

Trust that your purpose will grow as you keep showing up for your own life.

You are allowed to feel good again.

You are allowed to build something beautiful from everything you've survived.

This is your time to claim it.

Reflection | Affirmation | Prayer | Action

Cultivating Joy and Purpose

Reflection Questions

1. What does success look like for you—not anyone else?
2. How do you want your home to feel for you and your children?
3. What small joys have you been denying yourself because you were in survival mode?
4. What is one purpose that keeps you moving forward?

Affirmations

I am worthy of joy, rest, and purpose.

My story matters, and so does my healing.

Each day, I create more space for peace and delight.

I am allowed to dream new dreams.

God is guiding me toward the life I deserve.

Prayer

Dear God, Thank You for carrying me through the dark seasons. Help me to open my heart to joy again.

Show me the purposes You planted in me long before I could see them.

Fill my days with moments of peace and hope.

Teach me to celebrate the woman I'm becoming. Amen.

Action Step: Claim Your Vision

Take 10 minutes to write out your vision of thriving. Use this prompt:

"My life feels peaceful, joyful, and free when..."

Examples:

- "My life feels peaceful when I wake up without fear."
- "My life feels joyful when my kids and I dance in the kitchen."
- "My life feels free when I no longer owe anyone an explanation."

Keep this statement visible. Let it guide your choices and remind you of the life you are building. This is your compass.

Closing Prayer for Part IV

God, Thank You for the gift of new beginnings.

Thank You for showing me that thriving is possible, even here, even now.

Bless this season of my life with clarity, strength, and purpose.

Help me trust that every small step matters.

Let my home, my heart, and my children be covered in Your love. Amen.

Part V: Staying the Course

Chapter 18: Navigating Setbacks Without Losing Ground

Life isn't a straight line.

There will be days when chronic illness flares up, when your kids test boundaries, or when loneliness knocks hard on your door.

Setbacks don't mean failure—they're simply part of the journey.

When you hit a rough patch, try this:

- Pause and breathe before reacting.
- Adjust your expectations—today might not look like yesterday.
- Reach out to someone who understands your struggle.

Celebrate small wins, even if they seem tiny.

Remember:

Resilience isn't about never falling—It's about getting up one more time than you fall.

For most of us, resilience starts by default—but what if you chose to embrace it?

I've learned to treat my lows like they're just a different kind of high—an opportunity for clarity, for listening, for divine redirection.

Once I accepted that God is a mysterious being, I also accepted that He works in mysterious ways. Some of the darkest times in my life turned out to be the most necessary.

Did they feel unfair at the time?

Yes.

Did I feel like I was being punished or passed over?

Absolutely.

But here's the truth:

You don't always want what you think you want.

You want what God knows you need.

And that means being faithful even in the fog.

Even when you don't have the full picture.

Even when it hurts.

All work works.

Like Uncle G says:

"It's work on you until you become the person of reason whom it can work for."

No moment is wasted.

No setback is senseless.

If you don't see the blessing—

find the lesson.

If you can't find the lesson—

stand still until God reveals the blessing.

🐾 Reflection | Prayer | Affirmation | Action

Navigating Setbacks Without Losing Ground

Reflection Questions

1. What does resilience look like for you when life feels heavy?
2. How do you usually respond to setbacks—and how do you want to respond?
3. Are there past hardships that turned out to bless you later?
4. What lesson might your current struggle be trying to teach you?

Affirmations

Setbacks are not signs of failure—they are stepping stones.

I trust God's timing, even when I don't understand it.

I am learning, growing, and becoming stronger every day.

My faith grounds me when life feels uncertain.

Every challenge contains a hidden gift or truth.

A Prayer for Endurance

Dear God, help me stay grounded when life throws me off course. Remind me that even my hardest days are not wasted.

Teach me to trust the process, even when it feels like a pause or a detour.

Strengthen me to rise again and again—With grace, with faith, and with Your hand guiding mine. Amen.

Action Step: Create a "Bounce Back Plan"

Make a simple plan you can use the next time life knocks you down.

Include:

- 1 calming habit (deep breathing, prayer, journaling)
- 1 supportive contact (a friend, mentor, or safe person to call)
- 1 uplifting reminder (a quote, verse, or affirmation to read aloud)
- 1 way to nourish yourself (a hot shower, a nap, or a walk outside)

Keep this plan in a place you can access when you're overwhelmed.

Chapter 19: Protecting Your Peace and Setting Boundaries

Your peace is your power.

Guard it fiercely.

Setting boundaries can feel selfish or scary at first, especially if you've been taught to put everyone else first.

But boundaries are not walls of rejection.

They are acts of love—toward yourself and your family.

Say NO to:

- Toxic people or conversations
- Overcommitment when your body needs rest
- Guilt trips that pull you back into drama

Say YES to:

- Time alone to recharge
- Asking for help when you need it
- Prioritizing your health and mental well-being

Boundaries create the container where healing and thriving can happen.

You are not here to be everything to everyone.

You are here to be true to who God created you to be.

It will take practice, and some people won't understand.

But over time, you will see the fruit:

- more peace
- more clarity
- and more energy to show up for what really matters.

Keep showing up for yourself treat yourself with love and respect, others will have no other choice but to follow your lead, because nothing less will be tolerated.

🦋 Reflection | Prayer | Affirmation | Action

Protecting Your Peace and Setting Boundaries

Reflection Questions

1. Where in your life do you feel your peace being drained?
2. What boundaries have you been avoiding because you fear disappointing others?
3. How does it feel when you say "no" to protect your well-being?
4. What is one small boundary you can set this week?

Affirmations

My peace matters as much as anyone else's.

Saying "no" is not selfish—it is sacred.

I have permission to protect my energy and my heart.

Healthy boundaries make space for healthy love.

I am learning to honor myself without apology.

A Prayer for Strength and Clarity

Dear God, Thank You for showing me that boundaries are blessings.

Give me the courage to speak my needs clearly and without guilt.

Help me remember that I am worthy of respect and rest.

Protect my mind, my spirit, and my home from anything that steals my peace. Amen.

Action Step: Write Your "Peace Statement"

- Write a simple sentence you can return to when you feel pressured to overextend:

"I am allowed to protect my peace, and I don't owe anyone an explanation."

Keep it somewhere visible or save it in your phone for when you need strength.

Chapter 20: Cultivating a Support Village

Even warriors need a village.

You don't have to do this alone—no matter how strong you are.

Find your people:

- Trusted friends or family who lift you up
- Support groups for single moms or chronic illness warriors
- Mentors who have walked this path before you

Building your village takes time and courage.

Start small—reach out to one person today.

Share a little of your story, and see what grows.

And I'll let you in on a little hack I unlocked by accident:

My community was online.

I found different people to add to different areas of my life.

They were voices I could follow whose content spoke to me in ways that resonated deeply.

I had people for:

- Business and entrepreneurship
- Authorship and writing
- Gardening
- Parenting
- Cooking
- And even faith

Can you believe someone I never met in person helped lead me back to God?

I went out into the World Wide Web and curated my social media to give me what I needed:

- The advice I couldn't get in my close circle
- The encouragement that felt safe and nonjudgmental
- The inspiration to keep going

Because when you're the smartest or most motivated person you know, what can you do?

You find teachers and communities who elevate you.

If you can't find them in person—find them online.

My mentor doesn't even know I exist, but I follow, I implement, and I see results.

I can't wait for the day I can purchase his offers, because I know they'll take me to the next level.

Whether in real life or online, community is a bridge between isolation and thriving. Don't be afraid to cross it.

🕊 Reflection | Prayer | Affirmation | Action

Cultivating a Support Village

Reflection Questions

1. Who are three people you can count on for encouragement and perspective?
2. What kind of support do you most need right now—practical, emotional, or spiritual?
3. Are there online communities that could help fill gaps in your support system?
4. What keeps you from asking for help, and what would it feel like to let yourself receive it?

Affirmations

I am worthy of support and connection.

I do not have to carry every burden alone.

Community exists for me, and I am open to receiving it.

Every relationship that blesses me is a gift from God.

My story is part of a bigger story, and I belong.

A Prayer for Community

Dear God, Thank You for reminding me that I was never meant to do this alone.

Open my heart to receive the support You have placed in my path.

Guide me to people who will encourage, uplift, and walk beside me.

Teach me to be humble enough to ask for help and brave enough to offer it to others. Amen.

Action Step: Make One Connection

- Choose one supportive community—online or in person—and introduce yourself this week.
- Share a piece of your story or ask one question.

Your courage to connect could be the start of something life-changing.

Closing Prayer for Part V

God,

Thank You for carrying me through every high and low.

Thank You for showing me that resilience grows in connection and boundaries.

Help me stay faithful and steady when life feels unpredictable.

Fill my days with peace, my heart with courage, and my life with people who remind me I am not alone.

Amen.

Part VI: Growing Into Your New Self

Chapter 21: Growing Into Your New Self

    Every day you choose this path; you grow stronger and more sure of yourself.

It will hurt some days—just call it what it is: growing pains.

No one plans to stay small forever.

Just like children growing through those summer growth spurts—we grow through the pain.

And let me tell you:

I will take the challenges of becoming the new me, the new mom, over the pain of the old me any day.

That doesn't mean the new version of me is perfect.

It means she is committed.

It means she is working on herself, inside and out,

becoming the best version of herself—for her own healing and for her children's future.

Give yourself grace for the hard days.

Celebrate the victories, no matter how small.

Remember:

This isn't just about survival.

It's about becoming the woman and mother you were always meant to be.

Keep leaning into your truth, your faith, and your fierce love for your children.

You've come this far.

Keep going.

"I just can't give up now, I've come too far from where I started from.

Nobody told me the road would be easy.

But I don't believe He brought me this far to leave me."

—Mary Mary

🐾 Reflection | Prayer | Affirmation | Action

Growing Into Your New Self

Reflection Questions

1. What setbacks have tested your strength recently? How did you respond?
2. Where do you need to set stronger boundaries in your life?
3. Who are the people in your support village? How can you deepen those connections?
4. What new part of yourself are you most proud of?

Affirmations

I am growing into my purpose every day.

I have survived so much, and I am still becoming.

My growth is a gift to myself and my children.

I am allowed to change, heal, and start again.

God is with me in every season of transformation.

A Prayer for Growth and Grace

Dear God, Thank You for never giving up on me.

Thank You for giving me the strength to grow through what I've been through.

Help me to trust that every challenge is shaping me into who You created me to be.

Fill my heart with patience and grace when I stumble.

Remind me daily that I am loved and becoming. Amen.

Action Step: Build Your Daily Peace Plan

Write down three things you can do every day to protect your peace.

Examples:

- Take 10 minutes to meditate or pray.
- Say no to one request that drains you.
- Call or text a trusted friend.

Practice these daily for one week and pay attention to how your peace shifts.

Keep what works, adjust what doesn't, and keep building your own rhythm of calm.

Closing Prayer for Growing Into Your New Self

God, Thank You for guiding me through every season of my life.

Thank You for reminding me that growth is never wasted.

Help me to keep moving forward, even when it feels hard.

Keep my heart open to Your wisdom and my spirit anchored in Your love.

May I always remember that I am worthy, I am loved, and I am becoming. Amen.

Chapter 22: Embracing the Future with Intention

After the storms, the chaos, and the hard decisions—it's time to look toward the horizon with hope and purpose.

Your past does not define you.

Your choices today do.

Choosing to be a single mother by choice means

you're not settling—you're building.

You're creating a future that honors your strength, your values, and your dreams.

Ask yourself:

- What kind of life do I want to build for my children?
- What legacy do I want to leave behind?
- How can I use my story to empower others?

You don't have to come up with a plan to take over the world.

You just have to come up with a plan for today—and build on that.

Break it down:

- What do I want for me and my health?
- What do I want for my children's emotional, spiritual, and financial future?
- What do we need now—and what can we do next?

Don't get overwhelmed. Start where you are.

Work out today's problems and let tomorrow take care of itself.

"Don't waste today's energy worrying about tomorrow's problems."

You are no longer just surviving—you are planting seeds.

And God will provide the rain.

🕊 Reflection | Prayer | Affirmation | Action

Embracing the Future with Intention

Reflection Questions

1. What vision do you hold for your life one year from now?
2. What fears try to keep you from planning for the future?
3. What values do you want your children to inherit from watching you grow?
4. What can you start doing today that your future self will thank you for?

Affirmations

I am building a future filled with purpose and peace.

I trust God with my next steps.

I do not need to have it all figured out to move forward.

My present effort is shaping a beautiful future.

I am the author of a new legacy.

A Prayer for Vision

Dear God, Thank You for carrying me this far.

Help me to dream again—not with fear, but with faith.

Give me clarity to see what matters most.

Give me courage to move toward it step by step.

May I plan boldly, rest wisely, and trust deeply.

Amen.

Action Step: Choose One Cornerstone

Write down one thing that will be a cornerstone of your future.

Examples:

- "My children will grow up in a peaceful home."
- "I will become financially stable and prepared."
- "I will honor my body and health daily."

Put it on your wall, your mirror, or your phone screen.

Let it anchor your daily choices.

Chapter 23: Setting Goals That Matter to You

Now that you've reclaimed your peace, your identity, and your purpose—it's time to dream again.

Not someone else's dream.

Not society's checklist.

Yours.

It's time to set goals that reflect your unique vision. Don't worry about someone else's starting point. We're not all beginning at the same place—and that's not a bad thing.

Find people who've been where you want to go.

1. Learn from them.
2. Watch how they move.
3. Mimic the mindset, not the timeline.

"Be not conformed to this world, but be transformed by the renewing of your mind."

(Romans 12:2)

Your goals should reflect your life—not theirs.

Whether it's:

- Building financial security
- Pursuing education or a new career
- Creating joyful family traditions
- Deepening your spiritual practice

Make a plan that feels both achievable and meaningful.

Let's say your goal is to save $1,000.

You may not have that today—that's why it's a goal.

But you can start with $5.

Then $10.

Then more as you're able.

Progress is still progress, no matter how small.

Break big goals into smaller ones.

Celebrate every milestone.

Pro tip: The bigger the goal, the bigger the celebration can be.

🐝 Reflection | Prayer | Affirmation | Action

Setting Goals That Matter to You

Reflection Questions

1. What personal goal excites you the most right now?
2. What belief about success are you ready to let go of?
3. Who inspires you to keep going—and what lessons can you apply from them?
4. What's one small step you can take toward your goal today?

Affirmations

I define success on my own terms.

My goals are valid, even if no one else understands them.

I can start small and still go far.

Every small act of discipline moves me forward.

I trust that God will bless my work and guide my steps.

A Prayer for Motivation

Dear God,

You've placed dreams and goals in my heart for a reason. Give me the discipline to stay committed, the wisdom to move with purpose, and the faith to keep going when things feel slow. I trust You with the outcome as I do my part. Amen.

Action Step: Create Your First "Micro-Goal"

- Pick one small goal that supports a larger dream.
- Write it out. Give it a deadline.

Example:

"I will save $25 this week toward my $1,000 goal."

"I will walk for 10 minutes every day this week."

"I will write one page of my business plan by Sunday."

- Check it off when you complete it—and celebrate.

Let your confidence build, one small win at a time.

Chapter 24: Teaching Your Children Resilience and Love

You are the greatest teacher your children will ever have.

Not because you're perfect, but because you keep showing up. Because you refuse to give up. Because you lead with love, even on the hardest days. Your children are watching you more closely than you think.

- They see how you get back up when life knocks you down.
- They hear the words you speak over yourself.
- They notice the way you pray, rest, and protect your peace.

Whether you realize it or not, you are giving them the blueprint for how to love themselves and trust God.

Teach them:

1. How to express their emotions without shame or fear.
2. How to respect their own worth and the worth of others.
3. How to find joy in small, ordinary moments.

4. How to stand firm in their faith when life doesn't make sense.

Your legacy isn't just about what you leave behind in your will.

It's about what you build in their hearts.

It's about what you plant in their minds.

It's about the memories and lessons that will echo in them long after you're gone.

Some days you might wonder if you're doing enough.

You are.

You might wonder if you're getting it right.

You are doing more right than you know.

The truth is—your example will outlive any struggle you face today.

Because your children are not just learning how to survive.

They are learning how to rise.

How to believe.

How to start again.

That is a legacy far richer than anything money can buy.

So keep planting the seeds.

Keep loving them fiercely.

Keep showing them what resilience looks like in real life.

Because when you do, you set the stage for the next part of your journey:

Leaving a Legacy of Strength and Faith.

🕊 Reflection | Prayer | Affirmation | Action

Teaching Your Children Resilience and Love

Reflection Questions

1. What lessons do you most want your children to carry into adulthood?
2. How can you model self-respect and faith in your daily life?
3. What are some simple ways you can celebrate joy together as a family?
4. What seeds are you planting today that you hope will grow in their hearts?

Affirmations

I am teaching my children by example.

My love is a powerful legacy.

My children are learning resilience and faith from me.

Even in my imperfections, I am enough.

Prayer

Dear God, Thank You for the gift of my children.

Help me to raise them with resilience and faith.

Let my life be their lesson in courage, love, and honesty.

Cover our home with peace and joy.

Let the seeds I plant today grow into a harvest of blessings for generations to come. Amen.

Action Step: Create a Family Value List

Sit down and write out 3–5 core values you want to instill in your children.

Examples: Kindness, Honesty, Faith, Gratitude, Courage.

Post them somewhere visible as a reminder of what matters most.

Chapter 25: Leaving a Legacy of Strength and Faith

Your journey, with all its trials and triumphs, is a powerful story of strength.

Your life may not be perfect, but that doesn't mean it doesn't have purpose.

Every day you get up and try is another day you show strength.

Nobody sees the inner battles you face—the health decisions, the sleepless nights, the moments you go without so your kids can have what they need.

But you're not doing it for applause.

You're doing it so your children, and their children, will benefit from it later.

Legacy is not about wealth alone.

It's about wisdom.

It's about values.

It's about faith.

It's teaching your kids the power of saving and starting small.

It's showing them how to create boundaries that protect peace.

It's modeling what it looks like to trust God even when life doesn't make sense.

By choosing yourself and your children, you are teaching future generations what courage looks like.

You are showing them how to break cycles.

You are setting the standard for your bloodline.

Keep faith as your foundation.

Let it guide you through uncertainty and celebrate your victories.

Your legacy is alive in the love, lessons, and life you are creating now.

Reflection | Prayer | Affirmation | Action

Leaving a Legacy of Strength and Faith

Reflection Questions

1. What legacy do you want to leave for your children?
2. Which goals excite and motivate you the most right now?
3. How can you model resilience daily for your family?
4. What role does faith or spirituality play in your future vision?

Affirmations

I am building a legacy rooted in love, strength, and faith.

My children will benefit from the choices I'm making today.

I am breaking cycles and setting new standards.

My family is covered, protected, and blessed.

Prayer

Lord, Thank You for entrusting me with the gift of legacy.

Give me wisdom as I build a future for my children.

Help me set new standards of strength, faith, and love for my family line.

Let my choices today plant seeds that bloom for generations. Amen.

Action Step: Create a Vision Board

- Gather images, scriptures, and words that represent your hopes and dreams.
- Place them where you can see them daily.

Let this vision board remind you of why you are building and who you are building for.

Chapter 26: This Is Just the Beginning

This is not the end of your story.

This is just the beginning of your becoming.

You were never meant to stay small, hidden, or afraid.

- You were created to rise.
- To rebuild.
- To redefine everything you thought was possible.

You thought you had to wait for someone to save you.

You thought you needed permission to choose yourself.

But the truth is—you were always the answer.

All the courage you need is already in you.

All the wisdom you're seeking is already yours.

All the love you crave starts with how you love yourself.

Your past does not disqualify you.

It prepared you.

So as you step into this new season:

1. Give yourself grace when you don't have it all figured out.
2. Give yourself credit for every single step forward.
3. Give yourself permission to rest and still be worthy.

If you forget everything else, remember this:

- You are not behind.
- You are not broken.
- You are not alone.

You are exactly where God can use you—right here, right now.

Take a deep breath.

Close this book.

And open your life. The next chapter is yours to write.

🦋 Reflection | Prayer | Affirmation | Action

This Is Just the Beginning

Final Reflection Questions

1. What are you most proud of in this season?
2. What will you no longer carry into your future?
3. What new dreams are calling your name?
4. Who do you trust God is shaping you into?

Affirmations

I am ready for what comes next.

My story is not over—it is just unfolding.

God is with me in every step.

I am becoming who I was created to be.

I will keep rising, no matter what.

Final Blessing Prayer

Dear God, Thank You for guiding me through this journey of healing and becoming.

Thank You for showing me that I am stronger than I ever imagined.

Thank You for reminding me that my life has purpose far beyond my pain.

Help me trust You with my future as fully as I trusted You with my past.

Fill my home with peace, my heart with courage, and my days with gratitude.

May my story inspire others to keep going.

May my life be a living testimony of Your faithfulness.

May my children walk in the light of the legacy I am creating.

I trust that the best is yet to come.

In Jesus' name, Amen.

Closing Thoughts

You have walked through fire—and didn't burn.

You have cried, doubted, fought, and kept going.

Being a single mother by choice is not a sign of weakness.

It is a divine assignment of courage, vision, and deep love.

Your story is more than survival—it's legacy work.

So when you're tired, **remember:**

Every seed you're planting now will bloom.

Maybe not today. But one day your children will walk in the shade of trees you planted with faith and tears.

Keep going.

Keep shining.

You are the change your bloodline has been waiting for.

Prayer

Dear Lord, Thank You for walking with me through every page, every pause, every prayer.

Thank You for the strength You gave me to rise,

The clarity You gave me to release,

And the peace You are planting in my home and heart.

- I declare that I am no longer defined by my past.
- I am walking in newness.
- I am building something sacred.
- I am growing, healing, thriving—by Your grace.//
1. Bless my children.
2. Bless my home.
3. Bless my vision.

And when I get weary, remind me who I am and Whose I am.

In Jesus' name, Amen.

Scriptures for Strength & Provision

Philippians 4:13 (NIV)

I can do all this through Him who gives me strength.

Psalm 68:5-6 (NLT)

A father to the fatherless, a defender of widows, is God in His holy dwelling.

Matthew 6:31-33 (NLT)

Don't worry about having enough. Seek first the Kingdom of God, and He will provide for you.

Isaiah 40:29 (NLT)

He gives strength to the weary and increases the power of the weak.

Closing Prayer:

Lord, grant me strength, wisdom, and provision as I walk this journey. Help me lead my family with courage and trust in Your care.

About the Author

Shaundra M. G. Harris is a mother, entrepreneur, and advocate for women living with chronic illness and navigating single motherhood by choice.

Through her writing, she empowers others to embrace healing, faith, and resilience—no matter how imperfect the journey may look.

Shaundra is the founder of Shaun the Mom Publishing and is passionate about sharing real-life tools, encouragement, and faith to help others build lives they love.

She lives with her children in Michigan, where she continues to grow her own story of purpose and peace.

You can connect with Shaundra on social media @shaunthemom or visit her website for more resources:

www.shaunthemom.com or
www.warriormomacademy.com

The Warrior Mom's Guide™ Book Series

FOUNDATION: The Pilot Book

🤍 A Warrior Within, A Chronic Illness

The Warrior Mom's Guide to Sickle Cell & Chronic Resilience

My story of battling sickle cell while raising a family—woven with practical mindset shifts, survival tools, and advocacy.

📖 The heart of the Warrior Mom movement and the introduction to the series.

THE DEEP-DIVE SERIES (Books 1–10)

🤍 **The Warrior Mom's Guide to GhettoOCD™** (Home Organization & Cleaning)

Practical, real-life homemaking strategies for moms with chronic illness.

❀ **The Warrior Mom's Guide to Mental Wellness & Finding Joy in the Chaos**

Therapy, prayer, and emotional survival tools for weary moms.

🩶 The Warrior Mom's Guide to Single Motherhood by Choice

Reclaiming peace, health, and wholeness after carrying it all.

🩶 The Warrior Mom's Guide to Loving Unexpectedly

Guardianship, Fostering & Adoption with Faith and Fierce Love

Finding your voice, courage, and confidence in nontraditional motherhood.

🩶 The Warrior Mom's Guide to Generational Wealth & Family Legacy

Building wealth, purpose, and a future that lasts.

🩶 The Warrior Mom's Guide to Spiritual Reset & Chronic Faith

Faith after diagnosis, grace during flare-ups, and spiritual renewal when you feel forgotten.

⚫ The Warrior Mom's Guide to ZBB & Cash Stuffing (Finances)

Zero-based budgeting & cash envelope systems for sick-day survival.

🍃 The Warrior Mom's Guide to Homeschooling for the Homegirls

Practical tools for rest, rejuvenation, and chronic-illness-friendly homeschooling.

🖤 The Warrior Mom's Guide to Homeownership & Stability

Creative paths to securing a home with chronic illness and limited income.

🌿 The Warrior Mom's Guide to Living in Peace

End-of-life planning with grace: wills, medical directives, legacy projects, and restoration.

Find the books, companion workbooks, journals, planners, and more at:

www.warriormomacademy.com

Acknowledgments

Writing this book has been a journey of healing, growth, and empowerment.

First and always, I thank God for the grace, strength, and love that carried me when I could not carry myself. I thank God for guiding me through the darkest nights and lighting my path toward freedom and joy.

To my children—you are my purpose and my joy. Everything I do, I do with you in mind. Thank you for being my motivation and my greatest teachers.

To my family and true friends who stood by me in the hardest seasons, thank you for your prayers, your encouragement, and your belief in me.

And finally, to the women who came before me and paved the way—you taught me that survival is not enough. We were born to thrive.

To every mother reading these words—thank you for your courage to heal. May you find strength and hope in these pages.

This book is for every warrior mom choosing herself and her children, creating a life on her own terms.

Resource List

Support and Advocacy

- National Domestic Violence Hotline: 1-800-799-SAFE (7233) / thehotline.org
- Single Mothers' Support Groups (local and online)
- Chronic Illness Support Communities

Financial Help

- Benefits.gov: Information on government assistance programs
- Local Housing Authorities for affordable housing options
- Credit Counseling Services

Legal Resources

- Legal Aid Societies (search for local chapters)
- Family Court Self-Help Centers
- Guardianship and Custody Guides

Self-Care and Healing

- Meditation and Mindfulness Apps (e.g., Calm, Headspace)
- Therapy and Counseling Services specializing in trauma and abuse recovery
- Spiritual Growth Resources (local churches, online ministries

Reflection Journals & Worksheets

1. My Story: Write Your Journey

Use this space to write your own story—your challenges, your victories, and your dreams.

2. Financial Independence Checklist

- List my monthly income and expenses
- Open a personal bank account
- Set a savings goal for emergency fund
- Research affordable housing options

3. Boundaries and Support

- Identify areas where I need stronger boundaries
- List people who support me
- Plan one way to reach out this week

4. Vision and Goals

- What does thriving look like to me?
- My top 3 goals for the next year
- Small steps I will take this month

5. Daily Peace Plan

- Three things I will do daily to protect my peace
- Self-care activities I enjoy
- Affirmations to remind myself of my worth

www.ingramcontent.com/pod-product-compliance
Lightning Source LLC
Chambersburg PA
CBHW021157160426
43194CB00007B/784